How to Reduce the Stress of Being a Mum

&

Enjoy Time with Your Newborn Baby

Anya Nora

Published by Lulu

www.lulu.com

Copyright © 2010 Ganna Abdulakh

All rights reserved

Without limiting the rights under copyright reserved above, no part of this production may be reproduced, stored in or introduced into a retrieval system, or transmitted, in any form or by any means (electronic, mechanical, photocopying, recording or otherwise), without the prior written permission of the copyright owner.

ISBN: 978-1-4452-6359-5

Dedicated to my loving family,

Marcello and Stefano Nora

Table of Contents

Introduction

The first year of a baby's life seems to be the one that requires the heaviest adjustment from a woman. Not only do you have to build up practical experience on how to take care of the newborn, but you also face a dramatic change to your lifestyle. It is not surprising that most women find the beginning of being a mother a fairly stressful experience.

Over time, you will become an expert in motherhood and your life will reach a new equilibrium – except, why do you have to wait? Why not to find a way to reduce the stress and enjoy time with your little baby from the start?

To save you time and help you through the first months of being a mother, I wrote these pages. I will share with you how to make time with your baby more fun for both of you and how to make sure you do have time for yourself. The book will reveal what it takes to be a happy mother. It will guide you towards improving your relationship with your partner as well as your parents. The book will show how to keep yourself in good shape physically and intellectually. You will learn how to avoid sleep-deprivation, make your baby eat better and cope with your baby sickness. Finally, you will read about preparing for going back to work and choosing the right nanny or childcare.

One point to make before moving ahead is that I am not a perfect mum. I made some good choices and some bad choices. I am learning every day. This book is not about how to raise a better child. It is about how to be a happy mother. It worked for me. And by the way, my son is one of the happiest kids you can meet. I wonder: is there a connection?

One: A woman with an attitude

On the foundation of being happy

The book will go through practical ways to help you to reduce your stress and to enjoy time with your newborn. Some suggestions are easy to follow and some will require a commitment. But the key for these to work is to know that being a happy mother is not about what you do or what you have. It is about what you feel. It is all about the right attitude.

Like you, I have tough days when I have no desire or energy to smile. There are moments when I have no strength to deal with my kid's occasional tantrums that make heads turn. But most of the time I am a happy person, a happy wife and a happy mother. And what makes the difference is my way of thinking about my life.

I want to be happy and I believe that it is in my power to make myself happy. Luck obviously helps, but it is my effort that changes my life.

Is that the way you look at your life? If so – you will find this book very easy to follow and you will manage to cope with your stress and have a good time with your baby.

If you have not formed this 'I can make myself happy' attitude yet, take time to adopt the right mindset before moving ahead. Foster a sincere intention to make yourself happy and to believe that it is under your control.

I will give you an example. One mum has read this book and said “I do not know how you manage all the things you are talking about, I barely have time to sit down to eat. And it requires too much energy, while I am exhausted most of the time.”

How do I manage? I am not a superwoman. When I am getting too busy or too tired, I try to see what I can do with it. I review what keeps me so busy during the day and see if those chores are so important. Can I be more efficient? Can I try to do less in one day and pause to enjoy my time? How can I catch up on my sleep, having a little baby? Should I change the time I go to bed or should I nap during the day when my baby is sleeping, or is there something else I can do? I work through each problem.

To finish this chapter I want to ask you if you have heard about technology that lets you control a computer with your thoughts and emotions.[1] It is not only a reality, but it will also soon be widely available as a headset for computer games. Even today, gamers are able to move objects just by thinking of the action. This headset has 16 sensors that allow you to direct different movements such as pushing or pulling by just thinking about them. It can also detect about 30 different emotions such as excitement, tension, anger, etc.

Doesn’t it make you wonder if intentions and beliefs have a tangible force? Do not underestimate the power of your attitude. If you believe you can make your life better, it is very likely you will.

---

[1] See “Innovation: Mind-reading headsets will change your brain”, *New Scientist* (www.newscientist.com), April 2009.

Two: Adventure together

On learning on what matters & what does not

One of my favourite authors on self-motivation is Robin Sharma. In one of his books, *The Greatness Guide*[2], he talks about 'seven forms of wealth' which are important for reaching satisfaction from life: inner wealth, physical wealth, family and social wealth, career wealth, economic wealth, adventure wealth (meeting new people and visiting new places) and impact wealth (living for something greater then ourselves).

It is probably hard for you to be building your economic and career wealth during the first year of being a mother, but you are doing a lot for family and social wealth, and hopefully something for impact wealth by bringing up a new human being. We will talk about how to contribute to our inner and physical wealth in later chapters, but here I want to talk about adventures.

A lot of couples try to do all their exciting journeys before their baby is born. Great! But do not stop after you became parents. Choose a destination with adequate medical support and a moderate climate and take off for a new adventure with your newborn!

Travelling with an infant is more work but the trips with your baby will do all three of you a power of good.

---

[2] Robin Sharma, *The Greatness Guide*, HarperCollins Publishers, 2006.

For a mother, being out of your comfortable home, and having to adjust to the outside environment will help you to speed up the process of learning what is important and what is not. You will become less apprehensive. Changing your baby's nappies on the plane or in a park, or giving him a bath in a hotel sink will make you much less fussy and more relaxed about daily routine when you are back home.

Your partner will get an extra chance to bond with his baby and the three of you will discover a very special time to be a new family. Even your parents are likely to respect you as a mother from the start as they can see how well you can manage a holiday on your own with your newborn.

There is also some lasting benefit to your little one from adventures. Babies' brains benefit from variety in their experience. When you go sightseeing, your new family member is not going to remember a single thing, but the experience will not be wasted as stimulus from the trip is likely to increase his IQ. A study by Leila Beckwith of adopted babies discovered that the single factor that best predicted an infant's IQ score was the baby's exposure to other places and people both in and outside the home.[3] Clearly you have to avoid over-stimulation and keep an eye on when it is time to give your baby a rest. Do not plan your journey at the same pace as when you were travelling just as a couple.

When my boy Marcello was a month and a half old we flew to Italy. It is a good time for the first travel as usually after six weeks of age babies' night sleep lengthens. By that time, you as a mother will get better at breastfeeding and nappy changes. If your baby is suffering from colic or other

---

[3] See Lise Eliot, *What's Going On in There?*, Bantam Books, 1999, p. 448.

lasting unexplained crying, you may want to wait till eight weeks as that is the time when usually this extreme fussiness peaks.[4]

As the first trip went well for us, when Marcello reached two and a half months we took off on our three-week car trip across California. The twelve-hour flight to San Francisco was actually more comfortable because we had a newborn baby! Airlines provide a bassinet attached to a wall in the first row, so as a parent you get extra room for your legs, even in the economy class.

It is a pity that Marcello will not have any memory of beautiful vineyards of Napa Valley, giant sequoias at Yosemite National park and a stunning view along 101 Pacific Coast Highway. At the same time, it was so wonderful to see his wide-open curious eyes registering everything around him.

Did we have fun? Absolutely! It is still one of our favourite holidays we have done! It is amazing how many strangers started a conversation with us because we had a little baby! We met much more interesting people over our trip than we normally do when we travel as a couple. We even got invited over for dinner to a house of a private chef for one of the Hollywood celebrities.

Did we have any problems? Of course we had to make some adjustments. Once we had to run out of US superstar chef Thomas Keller's restaurant with our dinner in a doggie bag as our little boy could not stop crying. That was one of the most expensive take-away meals we ever had!

---

[4] See Dr. Marc Weissbluth, *Healthy Sleep Habits, Happy Child*, Vermillion, 2003, pp.138-160.

We learnt from that episode and did not go out for dinners and ate in the hotels most of the nights, though we could still try out restaurants during lunchtime when Marcello was having his day-nap. Now we laugh when we remember that night in one the top restaurants in Yountville, Napa Valley!

Be brave and have a new adventure, all three of you!

Three: Take your Mama out

On how to keep your baby busy and make new friends

Little babies are very difficult to keep entertained and spending the whole day at home is likely to drive you crazy. Your day is going to rotate around feeding, changing nappies and trying to soothe the crying, and at some stage you will get tired and stressed. That is why it is crucial to get out with your baby and do things together. Yes, you can – even with a three-month-old.

My suggestion is to make sure you have one activity per day scheduled for your baby. I think it is important to have a schedule as it will help you to get organised. When you know you have to leave home at 10 a.m., you must set a daily routine to get ready and prepare your little one on time. Otherwise, half a day may be gone and you do not even notice it!

You can join most of the classes when your baby is two or three months old. The earlier you start the better, as it will not only keep your child entertained and happy, but also use up his energy so as to give you an easier time at home.

If you live in London, the choice of things to do with an infant is amazing. I will give you the details of what I tried. Even if you are not from London, my experience will give you an idea what you can search for on the Internet for similar activities in your city.

If you live in the UK, it is worth checking websites of your local councils, which often organise free activities for babies and kids. As an example, have a look at *www.westminster.gov.uk/services/educationandlearning/childrensinformationservice/childrenscentre*.

And remember, as soon as you start going to the classes, you will find out more things to do from other mums.

Monday morning is for a baby music class. It does not mean that your four-month-old baby is learning to play the piano. It means that music is played to a group of babies. You may think that it is too early for your infant to enjoy singing, but it has been proven that babies are able to like and react to the music. Even a foetus can hear the sounds of the music while in the womb and remember it after birth.[5]

There is a wide choice of where to go for baby music classes depending on where you live and what you prefer. Search for Mini Ps (*www.minips.org.uk*), Monkey Music (*www.monkeymusic.co.uk*) and also Mini Mozart (*www.minimozart.com*). We went to Mini Mozart as there is a piano keyboard accompanist, while the main teacher plays violin, clarinet and percussion. Live music is always extra fun!

Mondays afternoon is for baby swimming. It is a wonderful thing to do as most babies love water; at this stage of their life it is the only environment in which they can really be mobile – they kick, splash, dive... The benefits of swimming classes to infants range from strengthening

---

[5] www.musica.uci.edu offers a collection of research articles on how music is perceived by infants, assembled by Dr. Norman M. Weinberger, a Research Professor in Neurology and Behaviour at the University of California.

cardio-respiratory functions to laying the basics of water safety.

We went to Little Dippers (*www.littledippers.co.uk*), but there are also Aqua Babies (*www.aquababies.uk.com*), Swimming Nature (*www.swimmingnature.com*) and many others. If you do not feel like committing to the set of classes, you can buy a DVD on Amazon called *Waterbabies* and go with your little one in the nearby pool that has a warmer area for babies, to try it out on your own.

Tuesday is for Mummy and Me yoga. Do not expect a heavy work-out either for you or for your baby. It is just gentle yoga for mothers and some rhymes and dancing for babies. When you are breastfeeding and carrying your little one all the time, even some stretching and twisting is very helpful.

The one we went to was at Triyoga Centre (*www.triyoga.co.uk*). The teachers are excellent not only at teaching yoga and entertaining babies, but also at creating a great atmosphere during the class. There are similar classes at The Life Centre (*www.thelifecentre.com*) as well as at some gyms.

Wednesday morning is for the baby-gym. The one near us is called Gymboree (*www.gymboree-uk.com*) which is open to babies from birth. All the classes are customised by age. You can help your child to learn crawling and walking, but more importantly, you will have a large safe space for your infant to explore. Bright colours, music and other babies will keep his interest up.

There are other places that run similar programmes such as Tumble Tots (*www.tumbletots.com*), Toddlers' World and others. The latter takes place at Swiss Cottage Leisure Centre, which is a communal sport facility, so it is a more economical alternative. If that is what you are looking for, check leisure centres run by a council in your area as they may offer some baby-gym set-up.

Thursday is for baby-massage. There are a lot of studies proving the benefits of gentle massage to infants. It not only improves the health of babies but also contributes to their mental development.[6] Apparently, there was a study where four-month-old babies received eight minutes of a massage daily and those babies improved their ability to recognise changes in audio-visual stimulus (one of the indicators predicting higher IQ later in life!).[7] So if you want your kid to become Einstein, check birth centres and hospitals that offer communal baby massage classes. We went to Triyoga Centre (*www.triyoga.co.uk).*

The idea is the same everywhere: baby massage is a class for mums with infants where an instructor shows you the proper way to massage your little one. After several sessions you pick up the main techniques which you can use at home going forward. I gave little massage sessions to my boy as a part of my daily routine. I am not sure that it will help Marcello to get a Nobel Prize when he grows up, but it definitely added some variety to our play and bonding time at home.

Friday is our rhyme time in the local library. At the beginning, these sessions are more useful for you to learn all those baby rhymes to sing to your kid when he is a bit

---

[6] Check www6.miami.edu/touch-research/ of the University of Miami's Touch Research Institute for some of the studies.

[7] Lise Eliot, *What's Going On in There?*, Bantam Books, 1999, p. 142-43

older. Then (in a few months) your baby starts to recognise some songs. I was astonished to see Marcello at around eight months doing the moves of "The Wheels on the Bus" when he heard the song.

Libraries often run such free sessions for babies and toddlers as rhyming is viewed as a building block for literacy. There are some studies that demonstrated a significant relationship between nursery rhymes knowledge at the age of three and successful ability to read and do spelling at the age of five and six.[8] The reason may be that nursery rhymes help children to learn how to detect the syllables or that rhymes provide a language rich environment from a very early age. Discussions among linguists are still continuing. However, what matters for us, parents, is that babies love rhymes and if we can sing them together it will help them to be smarter at school.

You would probably want to keep Saturday and Sunday free for you to take a rest and for your partner to bond with your baby. But if you want to keep yourself busy even during the weekend, you can add baby signing classes (*www.tinytalk.co.uk*) or French play-groups (*www.clubpetitpierrot.uk.com*). I may try those with my second baby when the time comes.

One thing to keep in mind when scheduling your classes – routine is good but keep it flexible! Do not stress out if you are running late or there is something else to do or you just feel like staying at home. Most of the classes are without subscription – you pay as you go, which means you can

---

[8] See Damon Syson, "Please don't kill poor Baa Baa Black Sheep", *The Times*, December 8, 2009.

skip some days or swap activities as there are usually more than one per day!

Four: Become an expert on being a Mum

On the importance of knowledge

A lot of the stress of being a mother of a newborn is due to lack of experience and often things we worry about are not important. Every mother becomes more relaxed with the second kid as the knowledge builds up. But how can we speed up the process of learning what matters and what does not? Reading books on parenting and talking to other mothers who have babies who are a bit older is crucial!

It sounds very obvious, but I was surprised to find out how little some of the young mothers read about being a parent. Most of them strive to be an expert in what they do professionally and read extra for their jobs, go to seminars, and attend training. But they view being a mother as the most natural thing and see no need to invest time into learning to be a parent. I found that the more you know from books and from other mothers, the more confident you become as a mother yourself. More confidence means you rarely panic and seldom get stressed.

To start your little library on parenting, here are some books I found valuable.

The practical one is from the 'What to Expect...' series that I found also useful during pregnancy. The relevant book in our case is *What to Expect the First Year* by Arlene

Eisenberg, Heidi E. Murkoff, and Sandee E. Hathaway.[9] This book is a kind of benchmark and the reference point you read month by month as your newborn grows. You will learn what to expect from your baby in terms of his physical, emotional and mental development. In addition the book goes through and answers questions that mothers usually have when their babies are under one year old. There is also a useful brief review of the health issues your baby may face and how to address them.

As the book covers a very wide range of topics, it does not go into any particular issue in depth and does not discuss much of the academic research done in the field of babies' development. If you are interested in this, have a look at *What's Going on in There?* by Lise Eliot. The book is an excellent synopsis of major scientific views on how parents can boost development of their children starting from birth (or to be precise from pregnancy). For example, you can find a scientific explanation about the benefit of breastfeeding or the importance of constant physical interaction with your baby.

Another quite interesting set of books is 'The Gentle Revolution' by Glenn Doman, which includes *How to Teach Your Baby to Be Physically Superb*, *How to Teach Your Baby to Read*, *How to Teach Your Baby Math*, *How to Give Your Baby Encyclopaedic Knowledge* and *How to Multiply Your Baby's Intelligence*. Glen Doman created The Institute for the Achievement of Human Potential in Philadelphia and his initial work was focused on brain-injured children. Gradually The Institute expanded its work

---

[9] Arlene Eisenberg, Heidi E. Murkoff, and Sandee E. Hathaway, *What to Expect the First Year*, Simon & Schuster, 2004.

on development of all children. You can find out more about their activities as well as seminars on *www.iahp.org.*

The programmes in the books require a certain dedication and I was not ready for such commitment. At the same time I picked up some simple and useful techniques from each of them that I can use when I play with my son. There are exercises that are suitable almost from the first day your baby is born! For example, from *How to Teach Your Baby to be Physically Superb*[10] (which has a lot in common with the Montessori approach), I learnt that gentle vestibular stimulation increases brain growth at the beginning of a baby's life. So the book suggests the best way to swing and carry your newborn so as to stimulate his brain development as well as improve his mobility competence.

From *How to Teach Your Baby to Read*[11] I learned how to make reading cards and from time to time I play them with my son. Not that he learnt much from it, but I feel that I am doing something useful with him and it makes me feel happier! My suggestion for you is to check these books on Amazon. Maybe you can be more persistent than me and your kid will start to read when he is two years old!

When you start thinking about the nursery for your baby (and from my experience it is never too early in London), you may be interested to learn about Montessori nurseries. Considering how popular they are today, as a parent you can make a more educated decision whether it is something

---

[10] Glenn Doman, Douglas Doman, Bruce Hagy, *How to Teach Your Baby to Be Physically Superb, From Birth to Age Six*, SquareOne Publishers, 2006.
[11] Glenn Doman, Janet Doman, *How to Teach Your Baby to Read*, SquareOne Publishers, 2006.

for your baby or not. You can get a brief overview of Montessori teaching from *www.montessori.org.uk*. If you want a more in-depth overview, go through *Montessori: The Science Behind the Genius* by Angeline Stoll Lillard.[12] The book discusses the main principles of Montessori teaching such as learning through doing, giving children choices of what they want to learn, teaching new concepts in a meaningful context versus abstract notions, and the importance of collaboration and order.

Even if you decide to go to a different type of nursery, you are still likely to find something useful in the Montessori approach that you can use in bringing up your children.

Among general parenting books I liked *A Child of Our Time: Early Learning* by Tessa Livingstone. If you talk to other mums, they will recommend plenty of other books they found useful. It does not mean, by the way, that you have to spend a fortune building up your own collection of books. Now you are likely to be going weekly with your baby to your local library for the rhyming sessions, so you can use these occasions to check the parenting section there.

Do not get discouraged by the number of books – you do have time to read them! Make sure you always carry one with you when you are out with your baby (luckily a pram has a lot of space!). When she falls asleep in a park or on a bus – you have something useful and interesting to do!

---

[12] Angeline Stoll Lillard, *Montessori: The Science Behind the Genius*, Oxford University Press, 2005.

Five: Fun things for Mums

How to enjoy the things you used to do before you had your baby

During the first months of being a mum I started to miss simple things, like going to see a movie or playing tennis or just rollerblading in a park. It took me some months to realise that I can do all the things I love together with my baby.

Ideally you should meet another enthusiastic mum, so you have a grown-up company for your activities. Probably you will have plenty of chances to make a new friend from the neighbourhood during those baby classes we talked about in the previous chapter.

Movies in a cinema are always more fun than at home. What a joy it was to find out that there are cinemas you can go to see a new movie with a screaming baby!

London has quite a few of these. To find the nearest to you, check the Internet for "Scream Cinema". The one I went to was the Everyman Cinema in Hampstead (*www.everymancinema.com*). The Electric Cinema in Notting Hill (*www.electriccinema.co.uk*) has "screaming" viewings. Usually the age limit for babies is 12 months as otherwise you will have to chase your little one across the entire cinema (which I tried and it was exhausting).

If you love live music, it is a bit difficult to find concerts where you can bring along your baby. But even that is not impossible. You can consider outdoor concerts which are not overcrowded (there are plenty in the summer!) You can also check nice boutique hotels which have some live music during the tea hour and are usually not that busy. I had a wonderful experience in the Rose Lounge at Sofitel London (*www.sofitelstjames.com*). Delicate music of a harp goes so well together with delicious Parisienne pastries and rose tea!

Outdoor sport was the thing I missed the most. I saw some mums running with pushchairs, but I knew it was not my cup of tea. Instead I was so jealous watching people playing tennis or rollerblading on a sunny day in a park!

Luckily I made a new friend who was also a new mum. She is one of those enthusiastic people who is not afraid to try new things. In a week we were on a tennis court with our two babies sitting in their buggies in the middle. Of course we could not play the whole hour non-stop or do servings, but we have managed some good rallies and had enormous fun. Next day we went rollerblading in a park. Our boys loved the ride and we had a great workout.

The point is to know what you like doing and try to find a way to do it. Obviously, baby's safety is the priority. Choose a fenced tennis court, so other players' balls cannot reach your baby. You should not rollerblade on slopes or cross any roads. Certainly it is not a good idea to learn a new sport when your baby depends on your balance or precision. Your stroller should be stable when it moves fast. It does not mean you have to buy a stroller designed for sport. I used my MicraLITE Fastfold (*www.micralite.com*) and it went very well.

Sometimes we like to see constraints that do not exist. We do not lead the life we want. Carl Gustav Jung[13] wrote once that "Nothing has a stronger influence psychologically on their environment and especially on their children then the unlived life of the parent". Now when you became a mother you have an obligation to live your life in full and be happy.

[13] Carl Gustav Jung (1875 – 1961) was a Swiss psychiatrist and the founder of analytical psychology.

Six: The only rule I always follow

How to find time for yourself

Nothing helps more to clear away the stress and tension than a quiet time on your own. As Eddie Cantor[14] said, "Slow down and enjoy life. It's not only the scenery you miss by going too fast – you also miss the sense of where you are going and why."

How to get this time when you have a little baby? When I became a mother, I made only one rule for myself that I always follow. When my son sleeps, it is MY TIME. I do not use this precious time for housework or other errands and chores. My rule may sound very obvious, but it is the only one which helps me to gain control over my time.

Most babies develop regular day sleeping patterns somewhere between twelve and sixteen weeks. It is likely your baby is going to have two or three naps during the day until nine months or so. The afternoon nap will stay till a kid is three.

I used my son's morning nap which usually starts around 9-10am to catch up on my own sleep. I still use my son's afternoon nap to read a book or play piano or whatever makes me more than just a mother.

[14] Eddie Cantor (1892 – 1964) was an American comedian, dancer, singer, actor and songwriter.

If you are worried when to manage all the housework and cooking, my solution is to learn to do things when your baby is awake. A cot mobile (not cell phones!), playpen or swing-seat will come in handy. Some of you can become a virtuoso and manage to carry your baby in a sling while tidying up, like women in some African countries. But I never managed to do such wonders and my secret is that I set up realistic expectations for myself (everything takes longer) and do not plan to do a complete clean up of my place or cook for a party. If you cannot get help with cleaning, leave the vacuum cleaning and washing for weekends when your husband is around.

To take maximum advantage of your baby's sleep, you have to plan the day a bit more. For example, I do not schedule any baby activities too close to the day nap time as I want to be at home for most of my son's sleep.

One word of caution: I do not suggest spending all the time your baby is awake cleaning and cooking. Learn to set aside time to play with your baby as it will keep him happy as well as boost his development. There is more about this later in the book.

To have two or three hours per day of quality time for yourself is a luxury not many people can afford. Being at home with a new baby gives you this precious opportunity. Do not lose it.

Seven: In a healthy body - a healthy spirit

On the importance of looking well and how to achieve it

When a woman is content about the way she looks, she feels happy and is less susceptible to stress. For a start, try not to use your newborn as an excuse for letting yourself go. Just few simple steps can make a difference.

It is easier to commit to little things. I am trying to spend 10-15 minutes every day doing my workout. The key point here is “I am trying”. If I miss it out for a couple of days, I do not get stressed out about it. Even four or five times a week make a visible difference. To keep your commitment, try to schedule your sessions at a similar time (e.g. before breakfast), so it becomes a routine. And of course, it is important to find a workout that you enjoy and that works for your body.

Six weeks after going through childbirth, I started with a DVD, *Postnatal Rescue* by Erin O’Brien. It builds up intensity gradually, so you can move through as your body strengthens after the labour. Later in the year I moved to *10 Minute Solution - Target Toning*. There are plenty of other titles on Amazon, so you can choose what works for you. The main point is to be realistic and start with short sessions.

In addition, once a week you can leave your baby with your husband for an evening after his work or for a couple of hours during a weekend to have a proper gym class/yoga/Pilates/swim or whatever keeps you fit.

Also find some gym or yoga centre nearby which has a wide range of drop-in classes in the evening or week-end. Remember the good feeling after a long work-out – tired and happy? The reason is that our brain releases endorphins when we exercise which makes us feel good. In addition, research by Emma Cohen at Oxford University[15] suggests that to exercise in a synchronised group may increase your tolerance for pain and make you work out for longer that you would have done otherwise on your own. So if you feel particular low after a long day with your baby, an exhausting class in a local gym will do wonders!

To complete my physical routine – I walk as much as I can. Taking your baby to the classes will offer you plenty of opportunities to do so.

Clearly no exercises will be sufficient if your diet is not healthy. I am not a supporter of particular crash diets or being hungry all the time. Just remember that neither being pregnant nor breast-feeding is a justification for eating the food you used to avoid before. You have to eat more, but eat nutritious food that benefits you and your baby (i.e. sweets are not part of such a diet) and go for lower-fat versions.

---

[15] Emma E. A. Cohen, Robin Ejsmond-Frey, Nicola Knight and R. I. M. Dunbar, "Rowers' high: behavioural synchrony is correlated with elevated pain thresholds", *Biology Letters*, September 2009.

It does not mean that if I crave a little chocolate I do not eat it. I do – but I make it a special treat rather than a regular habit. And make sure you always have healthy snacks like fresh and dry fruit at home.

I will not go through suggestions on how to manage to take a shower with your baby (a baby swing-seat helps a lot!) or reasons why it is important to care about what you wear even if you are not going to work but just going out with your kid. Remind yourself what a great boost to your mood it is to look at the mirror and like what you see. An extra few minutes of effort are well worth it!

Eight: There is more to life...

On the importance of keeping hobbies and friends who do not have kids

We talked about how important is to look well, but it is as important to be in good shape intellectually. A newborn baby demands enormous amount of time and energy. It is no wonder that gradually our thoughts and conversations are almost entirely dominated by this little being. You have to fight to recover your inner identity. Don't you feel better about yourself when other people find you an interesting person to talk to? So avoid becoming a boring person who only talks about babies. Intellectual curiosity is harder to maintain when you are taking care of a newborn, but there is a way.

I talked previously about how important it is to read books on baby's development, but make sure that it is not the only reading you do. For example, I make a commitment that only every third book I read is about children. I always make sure I catch up on the news and read good books not related to motherhood.

Another important point is to keep in touch with your friends who do not have kids. And what is more important, when you meet them – do not talk about babies! That will also help you to get invitations to parties other than babies' birthday parties!

If all my suggestions at these stage start to sound as too much work or impossible to do – remember Seneca[16]: “It is not because things are difficult we do not dare; it is because we do not dare that they are difficult”. I am trying to do things. And if there is a day I feel tired I drop all my plans and take a nap next to my sleeping son. That is the beauty of being a mum at home as you are the boss – at least when your baby is asleep.

[16] Seneca (c. 4 BC – AD 65) was a Roman Stoic philosopher

Nine: How to make play time at home more fun

On what you can do at home with your baby to drive his development and to have fun

During the first several months of becoming a mum, I struggled to find what to do together with my son at home. Marcello did not care much about my fairy-tales and his attention span towards new toys did not last more than few minutes. That is why baby classes were of great help – they kept Marcello entertained. But back home I was facing the same challenge – what can we do together? A couple of books and months later I understood that there are simple things that are not only fun to do with a baby from birth, but that also they boost his development.

To start with, you should change the perception of the time you spend with your baby at home. You are not a custodian, you are a teacher. Obviously you are here to safeguard this little creature, but more importantly you are here to give your baby the best foundation for his growth and development which he will build on through his whole life. In reality, it is in the first three years of a child's life that he is going to be absorbing everything from you exclusively. Afterwards his peers and the school become the main force influencing your kid's behaviour. When you remember that, it gives you a bit more enthusiasm and patience when you are tête-à-tête with your baby. Three years will go by so fast!

The simplest thing you can do with your baby is just talk to him. Extended research by Betty Hart and Todd R. Risley demonstrated that talking to babies not only encourages them to talk earlier but also advances their intelligence.[17] The rate of vocabulary growth predicts later performance in school, even at the age of 9-10 years. The simplified guidance from the research on how parents should communicate with babies is to follow five steps:

- *Talk* – use different parts of speech (nouns, verbs, etc.) and all tenses
- *Be nice* – approve and repeat, while making sure to avoid too many prohibitions
- *Tell about things* – draw attention to the present surroundings, talk about the past (what you did together yesterday) and what is going to happen next
- *Give choices* – ask yes/no questions and let your baby choose between two toys, etc.
- *Listen* – prompt responses and give time to answer (of course it will be just random babbling at this stage).

The "be nice" part is particularly important as negative words (such as "no", "do not") have a reverse impact on speech development.

[17] Betty Hart, Dr. Todd R. Risley, *Meaningful Differences in the Everyday Experience of Young American Children*, Brookes Publishing Co, 1995.

If you are particularly keen to stimulate your baby to start talking earlier, have a look at Dr. Fowler's work.[18] He developed a method based on parents anticipating each stage of baby's linguistic development. Thus, from the birth to three months, parents should do vocalization, playing with syllables and their different combinations. Starting at three months, parents should do "labelling" of objects around the baby, especially those that draw his attention. Gradually labels should expand to other parts of speech (i.e. pronouns, adverbs, etc.). From nine months, you should introduce phrases and sentences, building up their complexity gradually (like "this is a red car" expands over time into "this is a big red car"). Finally, starting from fourteen months, parents should try to engage their toddler in a conversation about events and surroundings.

Most of the suggestions are pretty intuitive, but sometimes we forget to keep up an effort to talk to our babies as we feel a bit awkward keeping a monologue for long. However, as the research showed, all the effort is worthwhile.

Another idea for doing something together with your baby is to listen to music, especially classical. There are a lot of discussions and research about the benefits of classical music that range from reducing tension to increasing babies' IQ. If you are interested in the subject, there is a wide collection of articles by Dr. Norman M. Weinberger, a Research Professor in Neurology and Behaviour at the University of California, at *www.musica.uci.edu*.

---

[18] William Fowler, *Talking from Infancy: How to Nurture and Cultivate Early Language Development*, Brookline Books, 1990.

An alternative way to explore music is to dance together with your baby. Get your favourite CD and see how much fun two of you will have! Infants benefit enormously from being moved through space (see Glen Doman's book on making a baby physically superb mentioned in Chapter 4).

I talked about benefits of massage to newborns in the chapter on activities. Baby massage is easy to learn and you can use quick sessions to enhance your bond with a little one as well as promote his physical and emotional well-being.

If you have a friend with a baby of a similar age to your little one you can start your own play group at home. Babies before 11-12 months do not really play with each other, but they will often find it fascinating to see another creature of a similar size. So, on the one hand your baby will have a new stimulus while you will enjoy a company of an adult who is going through a similar experience.

Learning to play again is one of the blessings we have as mothers; I cannot say it better than George Bernard Shaw, "We don't stop playing because we grow old; we grow old because we stop playing".

Ten: For better, for worse...until death do us part

On happy marriages and hard work

So far we have mainly talked about how you manage the change to being a parent. But it takes three to have a full family, and this third member has a lot of influence on your level of stress and happiness.

It seems that the most common issue women have with their partners after having a child is that men become terribly annoying. Of course I am not serious, but there is some truth in it.

It is very common to have some increased tension at home after arrival of a little baby. We can attribute it all to the hormonal changes postpartum as well as increased sensitivity due to sheer fatigue. But knowing the reasons is not sufficient to improve the situation.

How do we strengthen our relationship with our partner after we become parents? Let me share with you some tactics that can help you to maintain harmony at home notwithstanding all the big changes happening in your family.

Firstly, be direct in asking what you need from your husband. It is a common knowledge, that most men are not very good at reading the signals and when they try, they often get it wrong. He may sincerely think that, if you do not ask to help, you are happy to do everything on your own. Other times, he can be just lazy and unless you leave no room to escape he is not going to volunteer. So, just ask.

Secondly, do not feel guilty about asking your partner for help even though he spends a long day at work. Looking after a newborn baby is a full-time job which is quite exhausting. Obviously be sensitive and let him get rest when he needs it, but do not push yourself to the point when you just collapse. Your breakdown is going to exhaust him more than sharing chores with you after work.

Thirdly, when you do ask your husband to help you with the baby, show patience and trust. Allow him to make mistakes. If your partner takes twice the time to change a nappy compared to the time it takes you – be patient and not "too helpful". You do not want your spouse to feel inadequate. Gently pass some hints on how to do things better, but not every time he does something with the baby. Gradually, your husband will become a great father and you will get a trusty person to leave your baby with.

The fourth technique you should master is to listen to what your partner is saying without looking for the second meaning. Contrary to men, women are good at reading the signals and understanding the underlying meaning of what a person is trying to say. However, sometimes we are looking for the second meaning even if it is not there. Have you ever started an argument with your husband not because of what he said but because of what you thought he meant?

After our boy was born, my husband used to come home after work and ask "what you have been doing the whole day?" That would just drive me mad. I could see an implied question "You stayed at home the whole day, while I was working. You have not done much in the house. I wonder what you have been doing the whole day." So, offended and upset, I would go into a monologue about how he has no idea what a hard work it is to look after a newborn baby, that I had no time to rest, etc. Gradually I realised he really was just interested in knowing what I was doing during the day with the baby. My husband felt that he was missing seeing our son growing up and he wanted to know all the details about his day. So, when next time you speak with your partner, hear what he is saying without doubting that he is on your side.

The next policy to implement in your family is not to make your partner a target to unload your stress by picking up a fight. Sometimes, you can feel relieved if you let your negative emotions out on somebody else, but this is a short-term fix. Shortly afterwards you start feeling guilty and your bad mood catches up with you again. So, next time, when your baby has been crying non-stop for a while and you have burned your dinner, instead of letting it all out on your partner as he is twenty minutes late home from work, take a breather for solace. Even five minutes of solitude (maybe a quick walk or just gazing at the ceiling lying on your bed) can stabilise your mood better than arguing with someone you love.

Another important point is to be sincerely interested in how your partner is feeling and what are his needs. You cannot have a harmony at home if you only focus on your needs, feelings and emotions. Obviously, becoming a father is a big change. But your husband still has a big part of his life happening away from home. So find the time to listen to his concerns and give him the support he needs. Do remember to give a little hug and kiss not only to your newborn but also to your husband. Everybody wants to feel not only needed, but loved.

Finally, spend time together without a kid. I am not talking about the evening when you baby is finally asleep and your are so exhausted that the only thing two of you can think about is hugging each other on the sofa in front of the TV. I am talking about going out for a dinner or just for a coffee, depending on how much help you can get with baby-sitting. Being outside, and without your baby or your friends, gives you a chance of actually talking to each other. You can share your thoughts, discuss your plans, and just enjoy each other's company as you used to do before becoming parents.

Before having a baby myself I observed some couples with kids and I wondered how they could live like that. They argued about almost everything and one would wonder if there was any love left in those marriages. Only after becoming a parent did I realise how hard work it is to nourish a happy and loving family when you have a child. Our son is almost two years old and we are still work in progress. What matters is that we know our family is the most valuable part of our lives and we are ready to put in all our energy for it to flourish.

Eleven: Honour thy father and thy mother

How to manage the relationship with your parents and in-laws

There is a famous quotation of Oscar Wilde: "Children begin by loving their parents; as they grow older they judge them; sometimes they forgive them." I do not know at what stage you personally are, but if you do not want extra stress you have to learn to forgive now.

Having a baby means that you are likely to spend much more time with your parents and your husband's . If you have them near-by, you are blessed as you will always have emergency baby minders who are the most reliable in the world. At the same time, most certainly, you will have some differences about how to bring up children. Some of the discussion may get a bit upsetting for both sides.

Firstly, understand why your parents have a different view on a particular issue. I was amazed to find out how the recommendations of paediatricians changed over time. My mum was taught to make me sleep when I was a baby on my side to avoid choking on a reflux while asleep. I am taught to make my son sleep on his back to reduce the risk of sudden infant death syndrome. Thus, we agreed what is more dangerous and there were no more discussions on the issue.

Sometimes, your mother may know some methods passed through generations and it is your time to listen. It can be a mix of herbs to put in your baby's bath when he has some skin irritation or a way to soothe his crying. Just be open-minded and unless you have strong reason against the proposal – give it a try. You will keep your mum happy when she sees that you listen to her advice and you may learn something useful.

And there are moments when it is down to subjective opinion – like when to start solids or what is the best time for a bath. You are the mother and you decide how things should be with your baby. However, learn to distinguish what is really important to you and what is not. Let non-important things go. Life is too short to spend it arguing, especially with the people you love.

Twelve: Sick baby – how not to panic

On doctors, friends, Google and our emotions

The most stressful part of being a mother is when your baby is sick. As a little one cannot explain what bothers him, you feel helpless and desperate.

Obviously, nothing is better than professional help. So, you should always have a list of emergency numbers to call for a doctor as well as the address of the nearest emergency room.

However, for extra comfort, you should try to develop a relationship with a private doctor who you can call if something goes wrong at any day of the week or any hour. Ask your friends with babies if they know a paediatrician or an experienced nurse who gives his/her mobile and does home visits. When my son was about five months old he caught a virus. After 11 p.m. he started vomiting so severely that I just panicked and did not know what to do. Having a doctor I could call at that hour was such a relief. In ten minutes I knew how to help Marcello and everything passed smoothly.

As a new mum, you are also going to have a lot of minor concerns about your baby's health, like "why my baby's head is so often hot and sweating" or "why his hands are so cold all the time". Infants go through a lot of similar issues and most of them are quite normal. So, it is better not to worry about everything on your own, but ask your friends with slightly older babies. It can be helpful even to check the Internet as there are plenty of sites with mum's discussion boards such as *www.mumsnet.com* or *www.angelsandurchins.co.uk*. So instead of getting worried just pick up a phone or *Google* it!

One more point to make is that it is very important to control your anxiety when your baby is sick. Babies can feel their mummy's emotions, and your reassurance will be much more helpful to your little one. There was a range of studies that demonstrated how sensitive infants are. One of the studies showed that when a mother is distressed and her body stiffens, the infant in her arms will experience distress as well.[19] I had experienced that myself. After my son received his first immunization I was so tense that he cried for almost an hour. When in a month we came for the second immunization, I stroked him comfortingly and handled it with a smile. Marcello was happily babbling a few minutes after the shot.

No mother wants her baby to be sick, but do not worry about it in advance. Just be prepared. I like one of the quotes from Buddha's teachings, "The secret of health for both mind and body is not to mourn for the past, nor to worry about the future, but to live the present moment wisely and earnestly."

---

[19] Elaine Hatfield, John T. Cacioppo, Richard L. Rapson, *Emotional Contagion*, Cambridge University Press 1994, p.83-84

Thirteen: Non-eating disorders

On how to manage the stress of feeding your baby

After five-six months of being a mum you will face a new challenge as your baby is ready to start solid food. Choosing the best food and dealing with a fussy eater may cause some extra stress. What is the best food for your child and how to make him/her eat?

Firstly, try yourself the food you are giving to your baby. Even some organic jar food I tasted was pretty appalling. I am not talking about lack of sugar and salt which you have to avoid for at least the first year of your baby's life. I mean that the taste did not have anything in common with the ingredients it is supposed to be made of. So why do you expect your little one to like it?

My answer to make my baby interested in eating is to cook him fresh food myself. It does not take as much time as you may think, you know exactly what goes into it and you can make sure that the food is fresh. Even trusted brands may disappoint. Just remember a recent story (May 2009) that one of the baby-food giants was forced to discontinue a baby biscuits range after a major study found the cookies contained hydrogenated fat.

If you feel the same way and want to cook for your baby at home, I can assure you that it is not going to be too time-consuming or stressful.

Get a good baby cooker (like Beaba from Amazon) that can steam fruit and vegetables, blend them and switch off itself automatically. The first solid food you are going to cook for your baby will take 10-15 min. Cook enough food for two days – the food will remain fresh over that period and you have a day off from cooking. It is useful to have a good cook-book for baby food (like those of Annabel Karmel) so you can look up what to do with the stuff in your fridge.

And if you are lucky and you have a good girlfriend with a baby who you see often, you can do cooking in turns for both kids as they eat so little that you will have leftovers every time anyway, but in this case you will cook only twice per week.

As with everything – do not become too strict about your rules. When I am in a hurry or travelling, I buy prepared organic baby food. It is good to have a back up! But I make sure it does not happen too often.

There are also little snacks for babies from eight months onwards that are easy to carry in your handbag when you are out with your little one. I like all those cookies and fruit bars from Organix probably as much as my son and I always have some with me. But again, they are not a substitution for a home-made meal or fruit snack.

Even you are the best and the most imaginative cook in the world, there are going to be days when your kid does not appreciate your effort and refuses to eat anything. Remember that in most cases babies have a very good self-regulating mechanism. Some days they eat a lot, some days almost nothing. Make sure you offer a variety of tastes, shapes and temperatures of food to understand what your baby likes and ensure that he has a full vitamin intake. If there are days he barely touches food – relax and do not get stressed as there is nothing to worry about (unless your baby is losing weight or is not well). I never force my son to eat and he is still a happy, chubby fellow!

Fourteen: Sleeping time – how stressful can that be?

How to manage sleeping habits

Proper rest is one of the keystones for reducing stress. The good news is that having a baby does not mean inevitably that you are going to be deprived of your sleep.

There are different techniques to make you baby sleep through the night. One of the most popular books on the subject is Gina Ford's *The New Contented Little Baby Book.*[20] The idea in brief is to follow a very strict routine on feeding and putting to bed and waking up your baby. You are guided how to increase time between feeds (like at what part of the day you should give more milk to your baby), how to set your baby's environment to make her sleep overnight (i.e. have complete darkness in the bedroom during her sleep) and how to fight any resistance from your kid (for example, you should avoid any eye-contact or cuddling if the baby wakes up during the night), etc.

I picked up some useful tips from the book, but I was not ready to become strict with my newborn as I wanted just to cuddle him all the time and respond whenever he cried. So I chose to stay flexible to avoid stress for both me and my son. The drawback of such a decision is that I did not have uninterrupted night sleep for the first year. I still slept

[20] Gina Ford, *The New Contented Little Baby Book: The Secret to Calm and Confident Parenting* (2006 edition), published by Vermilion.

enough and was rested, but for that I had to adjust my sleeping habits.

Firstly, to make my life easier during the first four months when the frequency of feeding is high, I was leaving Marcello in my bed and was breastfeeding him without getting up. Overtime, I got so used to it that feeding was effortless and I would fall back asleep minutes after I fed him. If you are not comfortable with having your newborn in bed with you, you can put his cot near you as an alternative.

It is also very important always to catch up on your sleep during the day while your baby takes naps or go to bed early. As I mentioned in Chapter 6, most babies have two or three regular naps during the day from twelve to sixteen weeks. I used my son's morning nap to catch up on my sleep.

Later through the year you may get lucky and your child may learn how to sleep on his own. But if it did not happen (as in my case) and you feel that you want your uninterrupted nights back, you can start working on it.

Doctors suggest that you can try to influence your baby's sleeping pattern from four months onwards as the majority of babies develop an adult-like sleep cycle at this stage.[21]

You should start with setting up a bedtime routine so your baby will recognise that it is sleeping time. The routine may include giving a bath or listening to some quiet music.

---

[21] Dr. Marc Weissbluth, *Healthy Sleep Habits, Happy Child*, Vermillion, 2003.

Be consistent and allow 20-30 minutes for the process, so your little one has time to unwind.

The next step is to choose the right time to put your baby to bed. You have to learn to pick up signs when your baby is tired (e.g. becomes drowsy with slower movement and quieter) rather than overtired (e.g. rubbing his eyes and irritable). Your baby should go to bed before he becomes overtired. I made a mistake of putting my son to bed too late as he was going to sleep between 9 and 10 p.m. while getting up at around 9 a.m. That was very convenient for me as my husband could play with Marcello after work and I could sleep longer in the morning. But as our boy went to bed too tired, that was the main reason he kept waking up at night two or three times, even after his first birthday. After we shifted his bed time to eight, he started to sleep better.

Finally, to deal with night awakening, you have to let your baby cry. To help you through that process, you need two things.

Firstly, get yourself into a right mindset. Leaving your baby to cry in this case is not bad parenting. You are teaching your baby a very important skill of knowing how to fall asleep on his own. That means that his night's sleep will become unbroken and he will start his day better rested. There are also no indications that leaving your child to have a "protest cry" causes any emotional or physiological problems. You know that he cries not because he needs something (like food), he cries because he is not content to be left without your company. Wouldn't you ignore your baby's occasional cry when you put him in a car seat? You know it is better for his safety, so you do what is best for him. Teaching him a healthy sleeping habit is the same.

Secondly, make sure your partner is there to help you to teach your baby to sleep. Men are usually more resilient to babies' crying, so your partner will ensure that you do not give up half way through.

You can go straight to a cold-turkey approach and leave your baby complaining until he falls asleep. Alternatively you can try a more gradual approach of some crying before consoling. It is a very personal choice as everybody is different. The cold-turkey plan usually works faster, while the gradual approach requires more time. So choose what works for your and try to be consistent.

If you want to read more on how to improve the sleeping pattern of your child, I suggest Dr. Weissbluth's *Healthy Sleep Habits, Happy Child*. As a paediatrician and a researcher on sleep and children, he gives a good insight about the nature of sleep from birth to pre-school. He describes all the changes of sleeping cycles happening during the first year of a child's life as well as suggesting how to teach your child to sleep better.

Isn't it liberating to realise that with a bit of effort you as a mother can avoid sleep deprivation almost from the start?

Fifteen: The curious case of Benjamin Button

On the importance of being patient and how to control your emotions

The movie "The Curious Case of Benjamin Button" with Brad Pitt and Cate Blanchett is a wonderful tale about life and love. For me, though, it is first of all a must-see movie for parents. This adaptation of an F. Scott Fitzgerald story made me a better daughter and I hope a better mother as well. The idea of a baby born old and growing younger through life helps to visualise the relationship we have through our life with our children and our parents. When we were babies and when we needed our parents, they were there for us. When our parents get older, they need us and we have to give back their love and care. Your baby needs you now and you will need him later – so be compassionate, patient and loving. One day he will have to be the same for you.

There is scientific evidence that emotions are contagious and also that emotional mimicry can impact upon our feelings.[22]

The first point is pretty easy to accept. After a long tiring day, sometimes you think you have no more energy left, but then you hear your little boy laughing and the weight of all your troubles is lifted in a second! The reverse is true

---

[22] Elaine Hatfield, John T. Cacioppo, Richard L. Rapson, *Emotional Contagion,* Cambridge University Press 1994.

also: when my son has angry tantrums, I get distressed easily.

The second point about mimicry affecting our feelings is especially powerful as it means that not only do our facial expressions reflect what we feel inside, but also that there is a reverse process. You will feel happier if you smile. You are likely to get angry if you frown. It is a potent notion because it suggests we have some control over our feelings. Use this knowledge when you are stressed!

So the secret of feeling happier for a mum is to know how to make your little one laugh and how to join in. Do not be afraid to fool around jumping, spinning, dancing together. Learn your baby's favourite song by heart, so you can sing it to him when you are out. "The Wheels on the Bus" worked for us.

However, sometimes nothing works to stop a crying baby. In this case, not to get stressed, I do two things. Firstly, I remind myself that I should have the right expectations about my son behaviour, i.e. I do not expect things beyond Marcello's capabilities for his age. Secondly, I remember "The Curious Case of Benjamin Button" and try to feel compassionate and patient. See the world from your baby's point of view.

For example, it is hard to expect a nine-month-old to enjoy sitting quietly for a long time in a pushchair while you are having a coffee with a friend. If he starts complaining and nothing works to cool him down, I know it is time to go as he already has done his best. Instead of getting wound up, I take a deep breath, give him a kiss and we go for a stroll together.

It is not always easy to control our mood-swings or to be patient with a temperamental son/daughter. But it is possible to become better at it by practising. As mothers we need this skill even more as kids are growing up. Wait till you get to the toddlers' tantrums to see what I mean.

Sixteen: Back to work

On how to manage the separation

While you are pregnant, the duration of your upcoming maternity leave seems so long, but a few weeks into being a mum and you realise that time just flies. I was concerned with two issues almost from the start: when do I want to go back to work and who is going to look after my baby while I am working?

There is much academic and practical discussion about whether babies whose mothers work are not as happy as those who have their mummies at home. As you can guess, it is hard to generalise as it all depends how good the mother at home is versus how good the child-care set up is to help a working mum. Ultimately, what a baby needs the most at this stage is a caring and responsive adult, so she can develop a secure attachment.

As Eric Erikson (a developmental psychologist and psychoanalyst) put it, to have a healthy personality in the future, an infant must develop trust.[23] Parents are there to give the newborn a sense of familiarity, consistency, and continuity. That is the basis for the child to develop the feeling that the world is a safe place to be, that people are reliable and loving. If the parents fail to provide it, a baby can start to be suspicious of people and develop tendency to withdraw at a later stage. If instead an infant develops

---

[23] Erik Erikson, *Identity and the Life Cycle* (revised edition), W. W. Norton & Co., 1994.

trust, it is a foundation for mastering his environment in the future and being able to perceive the world and himself correctly.

Thus, it is not that important what you decide about going back to work; it is more important to stay responsive to your baby's needs and to provide continuity in his care.

From the stress-management point of view, I suggest that the primary factor for your decision when to go back to work should be what you think is best for you and your baby, not what other people (like your boss or friends) think. It maybe a month, it maybe a year – it is your choice.

I was in pain from the idea of having to stop breastfeeding and go back to work when my son was an infant. When he turned twelve months, I started to look forward to an opportunity to get out of the house on my own and get busy with work. Even so, the idea of working full-time was still daunting.

Choosing the hours you want to work may not always be an option. However, it is always worth asking for what you need. Your employer may agree to give you an opportunity to work part-time at least for a while after maternity leave. That would make your transition less stressful.

The second task is to choose a person to entrust your little baby. Take your time to do it right. When you start going to the babies' activities, look at different nannies there and notice those who you like. If you try to get to know them, later they could become available to work for you or they can help you to find somebody among their friends.

After you do make a choice, take your time to check the references from previous nannies' employers. Do not be shy; give them a call as you do not want any bad surprises after hiring a child-minder. In the UK you can also request a Criminal Record Bureau check (for CRB look at *www.crb.homeoffice.gov.uk*). When your nanny starts working with you, make sure you stay at home for the first few days as it will give your child a chance to get used to a new person and you will have an extra opportunity to observe her work. I would also leave some days as a cushion in case your baby or you are not happy and you need to find somebody else.

And finally, remember when you hire a nanny, you are becoming an employer, so take it responsibly. Create a workplace you always wanted to work in! Things like respectful treatment, proper pay, holidays, and work load are important if you want a happy and a loyal employee. A happy nanny will stay for longer and your baby will not have the emotional turmoil of losing someone he got attached to. To see how wrong the things can get, watch "The Nanny Diaries" with Scarlett Johansson.

If you feel more comfortable leaving your baby in a group childcare, there are also checks to be done. First of all, find out that a nursery is registered with the government regulator (it is Ofsted in the UK). If the nursery is registered, you can obtain a free report on the last inspection of the place to see if it meets all the essential requirements (*www.ofsted.gov.uk*). When you prepare your visit to the childcare centre before choosing one, make some basic checks:

- Is the atmosphere friendly and are the kids playing happily together and talking to the staff?
- Who is going to be your childminder every day?
- Is the place clean and safe for children (emergency exits, etc)?
- Is there sufficient staff (check number of children per childminder)?
- Can you meet other mums and dads whose children are in this nursery to ask about their experience?

No matter if you choose to hire a nanny or take your child to a nursery, observe your child's behaviour to see how he deals with the change. Considering that at this age your baby cannot communicate any complaints, your intuition and observation are the only things you can rely on to see if you have made a good choice.

I wanted to finish this chapter about getting back to work by letting you know what kids think about their mothers working. There was a survey of one thousand children aged between eight and seventeen asking what they wanted from their moms. Only 10% answered "more time", while the most common reply (34%) was "I want my mom to be less stressed and tired".[24] So if you decide to go back to work as that is what makes you feel more fulfilled, stop feeling guilty and having regrets. Your family wants you to be happy.

---

[24] Marcus Buckingham, *Find Your Strongest Life – What the Happiest and Most Successful Women Do Differently*, Thomas Nelson, 2009

Epilogue

There are never going to be enough books to answer all the questions that parents face. And there is no need to know all the answers. Every mother has her own way to be the best. My credo is to know what matters, to take a break when you need one, to see things from your kid's point of view and stay open-minded. What do you think?

If you like to share your experience or knowledge or give your feedback on the book – I will be very happy to hear from you at anya.nora.london@googlemail.com.

Acknowledgements

I am very grateful to my friends Giovanna Meire and Natasha Bowes, who took time to read a draft of this book and helped me to improve it. Giovanna's little boy Ethan is my son's friend and four of us have done a lot things together. Giovanna is the one who inspires me to try out new things all the time.

Natasha is expecting a little girl and she is about to discover all the challenges that a new mother faces during the first year. Her comments and views on the book were extremely valuable.

I would like to express my gratitude to Aidan Curran and Alan Wallace for proofreading these pages as without them you would not enjoy this book as much as I hope you did.

Finally, I give my very special thanks to my husband, Stefano, who was not only my passionate supporter but also my strictest critic. He made this book possible.

Index